THE BUSINESS MOGUL MATRIX

The Entrepreneur's Blueprint For Success in a Disruptive Economy

By Myra Wallace-Walker

ISBN: 9798312323023

MESSAGE FROM THE AUTHOR

Entrepreneurship is not just a business journey—it's a test of faith, discipline, and perseverance. **Faith** is the anchor that keeps you steady when the storms of uncertainty rage. It is the belief in your vision, when the numbers don't add up and the doors seem to close. Without faith, the weight of setbacks can crush the spirit, but with it, obstacles become stepping stones, and impossibilities turn into opportunities. When you trust that your purpose is bigger than your problems, you develop the resilience to push forward, knowing that your breakthrough is on the other side of your endurance.

But faith must be paired with **discipline** and **perseverance**. Discipline is the daily commitment to excellence, the willingness to do the hard work even *when motivation fades.* It's the ability to manage your time, resources, and mindset with precision, understanding that consistency creates momentum. Perseverance, is the refusal to quit when things get tough. Every great entrepreneur has faced rejection, loss, and moments of doubt, but what separates success from failure is the decision to keep going. When you merge faith, discipline, and perseverance, you become unstoppable—capable of weathering any storm.Think of ***The Business Mogul Matrix*** as a resource tool, to help you become triumphant as an entrepreneur in today's disruptive economy.

TABLE OF CONTENTS

INTRODUCTION

Why This Book? Why Now?

The United States economy is constantly evolving, and for Black and Brown entrepreneurs, the challenges are often compounded by systemic barriers, limited access to capital, and a rapidly changing business landscape. ***The Business Mogul Matrix*** is a unique guide, a strategic playbook designed to help marginalized entrepreneurs not only survive but thrive in an unpredictable economy. This book provides real-world solutions, actionable insights, and resourceful strategies for starting, operating, and expanding a business with minimal resources.

This book will focus on practical steps for navigating economic disruptions, leveraging community resources, mastering financial literacy, and building sustainable, recession-proof businesses. Each chapter provides a structured framework to empower readers with knowledge, strategy, and resilience.

CHAPTER 1

Know Who You Are &
Know Who They Are

As an entrepreneur one of the consistent issues you will face is how to navigate the human nature of those you encounter, like the various personalities you connect with, be it your employee, your consultant, a vendor or even your customers. The bottom line is, as the person behind the business, it is up to you to discern how to deal with each individual, as your encounters will be as different as the individuals you face. So before we dive into the nuts and bolts of this guide, let us first take a quick glance at four personality types and while we're at it, you might even discover which personality you best align with, it's very possible you may be a mix of two.

Many years ago, while running my manufacturing business a dear friend recommended a book by *Florence Littauer* entitled ***The Personality Tree.*** "I highly recommend this book if you would like a deeper dive into the subject of understanding how to have healthy interaction with others who may be different than yourself". For now, I will use a few points from her book as a point of reference in recognizing the different personality types you will encounter as an entrepreneur and in social settings.

The Personality Tree outlines four distinct personality types (*Sanguine, Choleric, Melancholic, Phlegmatic*) that influence our behaviors, preferences, and perhaps even the way they dress. Each quadrant reflects a unique style type shaped by personality traits and since I have an extensive background in fashion, I've included some visual clues to look for in their fashion statement. Below is an overview of how personality impacts style choices, including clothing preferences, color tendencies, and of course their entrepreneurial strengths.
Understanding your personality quadrant can help refine your style with your inner self, allowing you to feel both authentic and confident in your choices.

The Sanguine (Expressive and Energetic)

- Personality Traits: Outgoing, fun-loving, social, spontaneous, and lively.
- Style Overview: The Sanguine dresser loves to express themselves through bold, eclectic, and attention-grabbing fashion.
    - What They Wear: Statement pieces, trendy outfits, and mix-and-match ensembles with vibrant patterns.

- Colors: Bright, cheerful tones like yellows, oranges, hot pinks, and electric blues.
- Accessories: Large, bold jewelry, funky sunglasses, and colorful scarves or shoes that add flair.

- Impact of Personality: Their outgoing nature leads them to experiment and seek pieces that make them stand out. They enjoy fashion as a playful and creative outlet.
- Entrepreneurial Strength-(The Enthusiast) – Sanguines thrive in dynamic, **people-oriented** environments that allow them to use their charisma and social skills. Ideal entrepreneurial pursuits include event planning, entertainment, sales, public speaking, social media influencing, and hospitality businesses. Their ability to network and inspire makes them excellent brand ambassadors and marketers.

The Choleric (Bold and Commanding)

- Personality Traits: Driven, goal-oriented, assertive, and practical.
- Style Overview: Choleric individuals prefer polished, tailored, and professional looks that exude authority and confidence.
    - What They Wear: Power suits, structured blazers, sharp trousers, and classic pumps or oxfords.

  - Colors: Strong, commanding hues like black, navy blue, crimson, and dark green.
  - Accessories: Minimal but impactful—such as a sleek watch, a statement belt, or a classic leather bag.
- Impact of Personality: Their need for control and efficiency is reflected in clean lines and well-structured outfits. They avoid frivolous or overly casual clothing, focusing on timeless staples that project leadership.
- Entrepreneurial Strength (The Leader) – Cholerics are **goal-driven**, decisive, and natural leaders, making them suited for high-stakes, strategic ventures. They excel in industries like business consulting, tech startups, leadership coaching, real estate development, and franchise ownership. Their ability to take risks and drive teams forward helps them build scalable, high-impact businesses.

The Melancholic (Thoughtful and Refined)

- Personality Traits: Sensitive, introspective, detail-oriented, and artistic.
- Style Overview: Melancholic individuals lean toward elegant, understated, and timeless fashion with an emphasis on quality and sophistication.

    - What They Wear: Classic silhouettes, vintage-inspired outfits, and well-crafted fabrics like cashmere, silk, or tweed.
    - Colors: Muted and harmonious tones like soft grays, navy, beige, pastel pink, and lavender.
    - Accessories: Simple, delicate jewelry, leather gloves, or a structured bag.
- Impact of Personality: Their introspective and perfectionist tendencies make them gravitate toward cohesive, well-coordinated looks. They often prioritize quality over quantity.
- Entrepreneurial Strength (The Analyst) – **Detail-oriented** and perfectionistic, Melancholics succeed in businesses that require precision, deep thinking, and structure. They thrive in industries such as finance, law, research-based startups, content writing, fine arts, and specialty craftsmanship. Their dedication to quality and analytical skills make them excellent consultants, authors, designers, and educators.

The Phlegmatic (Calm and Peaceful)

- Personality Traits: Easy-going, dependable, and nurturing.
- Style Overview: Phlegmatic individuals prefer relaxed, comfortable, and practical clothing that matches their laid-back demeanor.

- What They Wear: Cozy sweaters, jeans, casual dresses, or versatile pieces like cardigans and loafers.
- Colors: Earthy and calming tones such as olive green, beige, soft blues, and browns.
- Accessories: Minimalist and functional—such as crossbody bags, simple watches, or sneakers.

- Impact of Personality: Their calm and steady nature translates to fuss-free clothing. They prioritize comfort and functionality over trends and are drawn to versatile pieces.
- Entrepreneurial Strength (The Nurturer) – Patient and harmonious, Phlegmatics do well in **people-centered** businesses that emphasize care, stability, and long-term relationships. Ideal entrepreneurial paths include counseling, wellness coaching, healthcare services, nonprofit organizations, sustainable businesses, and community-based ventures. Their ability to create trust and maintain steady growth makes them great in service-driven industries.

CHAPTER 2

The Game Has Changed

Pivot Or Perish

Economic shifts—whether global or national—are inevitable, but small businesses that remain agile, informed, and proactive can turn challenges into opportunities. By understanding macroeconomic trends, diversifying revenue streams, leveraging technology, and building financial resilience, entrepreneurs can safeguard their businesses against economic turbulence.

More importantly, small business owners must recognize that adaptability is key. While the economy may be beyond their control, their response to these shifts can determine long-term success. By embracing innovation, strategic planning, and a customer-first approach, small businesses can not only survive but thrive in an ever-changing economic landscape.

Small businesses are the backbone of the economy, accounting for nearly 99% of all U.S. businesses and employing almost half of the workforce. Yet, they are often the first to feel the pressure when economic conditions shift at a global or national level. Unlike large corporations that have deep financial reserves, diversified revenue streams, and political influence, small businesses operate with tighter margins and fewer resources. This makes them particularly vulnerable to economic disruptions—whether triggered by inflation, recessions, supply chain breakdowns, labor market changes, or geopolitical instability.

Understanding how these macroeconomic forces impact small businesses is crucial for entrepreneurs navigating today's unpredictable market landscape. Below, we explore key economic shifts and their consequences for small enterprises.

Inflation & the Cost of Doing Business

Inflation—the rise in the general price level of goods and services—affects businesses of all sizes, but small businesses are disproportionately impacted due to limited pricing power. When inflation rises:

- Raw materials and inventory costs increase, making it more expensive for small retailers, manufacturers, and service providers to operate.

- Wages go up, as workers demand higher salaries to keep up with rising living costs, straining payroll budgets.
- Consumer spending declines, especially for non-essential goods and services, which directly impacts revenue for small businesses.
- Interest rates rise, making loans and credit lines more expensive, limiting access to growth capital.

Larger businesses often have the advantage of negotiating supplier contracts, adjusting pricing strategies, and absorbing short-term cost hikes. However, small businesses must find creative ways to stay afloat, such as streamlining operations, leveraging technology to cut costs, and seeking alternative suppliers.

Recessions and Consumer Behavior Shifts

During a recession—defined by declining GDP, rising unemployment, and reduced consumer spending—small businesses often experience revenue declines and liquidity crunches. Consumer confidence wanes, leading people to cut back on discretionary spending, which directly affects restaurants, boutiques, beauty salons, and luxury services.

In a downturn:

- Businesses that sell non-essential products often experience severe revenue drops.
- Customers shift towards lower-cost alternatives or delay purchases, reducing demand for premium brands and specialty goods.
- Small businesses may struggle with cash flow as clients take longer to pay invoices, creating a domino effect of delayed payments.
- Credit markets tighten, making it harder to secure business loans, forcing entrepreneurs to dip into personal savings or seek alternative funding sources.

Surviving a recession requires strategic financial planning, including maintaining an emergency cash reserve, diversifying revenue streams, and strengthening customer loyalty through value-driven marketing.

Global Supply Chain Disruptions and Small Business Vulnerability

Over the past few decades, small businesses have become increasingly dependent on global supply chains for sourcing products and materials. However, disruptions—such as those caused by the COVID-19 pandemic, trade wars, and geopolitical conflicts—expose vulnerabilities in small business operations. Common impacts include:

- Shipping delays and higher freight costs, leading to inventory shortages and lost sales.
- Increased dependency on domestic suppliers, which may be more expensive but provide greater reliability.
- Fluctuating exchange rates, making imported goods unpredictable in pricing.

To mitigate risks, small businesses must rethink supply chain strategies, including nearshoring (sourcing from nearby countries), stockpiling critical inventory, and leveraging digital tools to enhance inventory management.

Hiring and Retention Challenges

National labor market trends—whether driven by technological advancements, demographic shifts, or wage growth policies—directly affect small businesses. Over the past few years, worker shortages, rising minimum wages, and changing workforce expectations (such as demands for remote work) have made it difficult for small businesses to attract and retain employees.

Key challenges include:

- Higher labor costs, especially in industries like hospitality, retail, and food services.
- Increased competition from larger companies, which can afford to offer higher wages and better benefits.
- Skills shortages, particularly in technical and specialized roles, making it harder for small businesses to find qualified workers.

To stay competitive, small businesses must adopt innovative hiring strategies, such as offering flexible work arrangements, up-skilling employees, and fostering a strong workplace culture.

Federal Policies and Taxation: The Double-Edged Sword

Government policies—ranging from tax regulations to stimulus programs—can either help or hinder small business growth. In times of economic instability, federal relief programs, tax credits, and grants can provide crucial support. However, shifting tax laws and regulatory burdens can also create obstacles.

For example:

- Tax hikes reduce net earnings for small business owners.
- New labor laws (such as stricter overtime pay requirements) increase operational costs.

- Government stimulus programs (like the Paycheck Protection Program) offer temporary relief but may come with stringent compliance requirements.

Staying informed about policy changes and working with financial advisors can help entrepreneurs maximize available benefits while avoiding potential pitfalls.

Geopolitical Events and Market Volatility

Global conflicts, trade tensions, and political instability can have far-reaching effects on small businesses, particularly those involved in international trade. Tariffs, sanctions, and trade restrictions can lead to supply chain disruptions, increased costs, and limited market access. Additionally, currency fluctuations can impact pricing strategies for businesses that rely on imports or exports.

To navigate geopolitical uncertainty, small businesses must:

- Diversify suppliers to reduce reliance on any single region.
- Stay informed about international trade policies.
- Consider localizing production to mitigate risks associated with overseas sourcing.

The business landscape has undergone a seismic shift in the past decade, largely driven by digital commerce, automation, and artificial intelligence (AI). These three forces have not only transformed how businesses operate but have also redefined the entrepreneurial playing field, creating both unprecedented opportunities and significant challenges, particularly for underserved Black and Brown entrepreneurs.

The Rise of Digital Commerce

Digital commerce has fundamentally altered consumer behavior and market dynamics. With global e-commerce sales expected to surpass $8 trillion by 2027, businesses that fail to adopt a strong digital presence risk obsolescence. Digital platforms like Shopify, Amazon, and Instagram Shopping have democratized access to global markets, allowing small businesses to compete alongside multinational corporations. For entrepreneurs, the elimination of traditional barriers to entry means they can launch and scale businesses with lower overhead costs than ever before. However, this also creates a highly competitive environment where differentiation, branding, and customer experience are critical to survival.

For Black and Brown entrepreneurs, digital commerce presents an opportunity to bypass historically exclusionary retail systems. By leveraging direct-to-consumer (DTC) models, social media marketing, and digital advertising, these businesses can cultivate strong customer bases without the need for costly brick-and-mortar locations. However, challenges such as access to capital, digital literacy, and algorithm biases in advertising platforms continue to pose hurdles.

The Impact of Automation

Automation is revolutionizing industries by streamlining operations, reducing costs, and increasing efficiency. From AI-powered chatbots handling customer service to robotic process automation (RPA) optimizing supply chains, businesses that integrate automation gain a significant edge in productivity. This shift allows small businesses to compete at scale, but it also raises concerns about job displacement and workforce reskilling.

For entrepreneurs, automation presents a double-edged sword. On one hand, it enables lean operations, reducing reliance on extensive staffing and minimizing human error. On the other, it requires an upfront investment in technology and systems that may not be financially feasible for all startups. Additionally, industries that have historically provided employment for marginalized communities—such as retail, manufacturing, and logistics—are increasingly automated, leading to the displacement of low-skill jobs. Entrepreneurs and business owners must adapt by integrating automation in ways that enhance their workforce rather than replace it entirely.

The Role of Artificial Intelligence (AI)

AI is arguably the most disruptive technological force shaping the new economy. AI-driven tools are redefining decision-making, personalization, and predictive analytics across industries. Businesses use AI for everything from targeted marketing and fraud detection to supply chain optimization and customer service enhancements.

For Black and Brown entrepreneurs, AI offers a chance to optimize business strategies, improve efficiencies, and gain consumer insights that were previously inaccessible. AI-driven analytics can help businesses predict market trends, personalize customer interactions, and automate tedious tasks, allowing entrepreneurs to focus on innovation and growth. However, AI also presents challenges related to algorithmic bias, ethical considerations, and data accessibility. Many AI models are trained on biased datasets that do not accurately reflect diverse consumer behaviors, which can lead to disparities in marketing reach, financial approvals, and hiring processes.

Adapting to the New Economy

To thrive in this evolving economy, entrepreneurs must adopt a proactive approach to digital transformation. Key strategies include:

1. **Developing Digital Competencies** – Investing in digital literacy and e-commerce strategies is essential. Entrepreneurs must become proficient in social media marketing, SEO, and data analytics to remain competitive.
2. **Leveraging Automation Effectively** – Small businesses should prioritize automation in areas that enhance efficiency without sacrificing customer experience. Tools like automated scheduling, AI-driven marketing platforms, and CRM systems can be cost-effective and impactful.
3. **Utilizing AI Responsibly** – Entrepreneurs should leverage AI-driven business intelligence

tools but remain aware of biases and limitations. Engaging with diverse datasets and ethical AI practices will help mitigate potential risks.

4. **Building Resilient Business Models** – The adaptability of business models is crucial in an AI-driven economy. Diversifying income streams, creating scalable digital products, and fostering strong brand loyalty can safeguard against market volatility.

The rise of digital commerce, automation, and AI is redefining the entrepreneurial landscape. While these advancements present immense opportunities, they also introduce new challenges that require strategic navigation. For Black and Brown entrepreneurs, digital transformation is not just an option—it is an imperative for survival and success. By embracing innovation, building digital acumen, and advocating for equitable access to technological resources, these business leaders can position themselves at the forefront of the new economy rather than being left behind.

Navigating Systemic Barriers

Entrepreneurship is a powerful vehicle for economic empowerment, but Black and Brown business owners often face systemic barriers that hinder access to capital, resources, and opportunities. From historical wealth gaps to structural biases in banking, real estate, and corporate partnerships, these challenges require strategic navigation. However, with resilience, knowledge, and community support, Black and Brown entrepreneurs can break through these barriers and build thriving businesses.

Access to Capital and Funding Alternatives For the Underserved

Traditional banking systems often impose higher loan denial rates and unfavorable lending terms on Black and Brown entrepreneurs. To combat this, business owners should:

- Leverage Community Development Financial Institutions (CDFIs) & Minority-Owned Banks. CDFIs and Black- or Latino-owned banks are more likely to support minority entrepreneurs with favorable lending options.
- Seek Grants and Venture Capital: Programs like the MBDA (Minority Business Development Agency), NAACP grants, and diversity-focused venture capital firms offer funding tailored to Black and Brown entrepreneurs.
- Explore Crowdfunding & Community Investing: Platforms like FundBlackFounders and Kiva help businesses raise money directly from supporters who believe in their vision.

Strengthening Business Knowledge and Networks

A strong network and continuous learning are essential to overcoming institutional roadblocks. Entrepreneurs should:

- ***Join Minority Business Associations:*** Groups like the National Black Chamber of Commerce (NBCC) and Hispanic Chamber of Commerce provide mentorship, advocacy, and funding opportunities.
- ***Participate in Business Incubators & Accelerators:*** Programs like Google for Startups Black Founders Fund and LISC's Entrepreneurship Center offer mentorship, capital, and resources to scale businesses.
- ***Utilize Free Educational Platforms:*** Websites like SBA.gov, SCORE, and Coursera offer free courses on business planning, financial literacy, and marketing strategies.

Overcoming Bias in Business Operations

Black and Brown entrepreneurs often face discrimination in contracting, hiring, and scaling their businesses. Solutions include:

- ***Supplier Diversity & Corporate Partnerships:*** Many major corporations that previously had supplier diversity programs are undergoing major changes with prioritize working with minority-owned businesses, due to the political directives of the current administration Entrepreneurs should seek partnerships that leverage the playing field giving access to marginalized businesses.
- ***Leveraging E-commerce & Social Media:*** The digital space provides an opportunity to reach global markets without traditional gatekeepers. Platforms like Shopify, TikTok Shop, and Instagram Marketing enable direct engagement with customers.
- ***Building Legal & Financial Protections:*** Hiring a trusted attorney, securing strong contracts, and understanding intellectual property rights can prevent exploitation and unfair business practices.

Advocating for Policy Change & Collective Economic Power

Systemic barriers won't disappear overnight, but collective efforts can bring change. Entrepreneurs should:

- ***Engage in Local & Federal Advocacy:*** Supporting policies that promote equitable lending, small business funding, and anti-discrimination protections ensures long-term systemic shifts.
- ***Collaborate with Other Minority-Owned Businesses:*** Cooperative economics—such as group purchasing, shared marketing, and joint ventures—can increase bargaining power.
- ***Encourage Community Investment:*** Initiatives like buying from other small businesses and reinvesting profits in the community to help circulate wealth and create generational impact.

Despite systemic challenges, Black and Brown entrepreneurs continue to innovate, disrupt industries, and build legacy wealth. By leveraging alternative funding, expanding their networks, adopting digital tools, and advocating for equitable policies, they can create sustainable businesses that drive economic empowerment for generations to come.

Turning Economic Disruption into Opportunity

Economic disruption is an unavoidable reality. Whether triggered by technological advancements, global pandemics, financial crises, or shifts in consumer behavior, economic disruptions challenge traditional business models and force industries to adapt. However, within these challenges lie immense opportunities for innovation, growth, and transformation.

Economic disruptions create volatility and uncertainty, often leading to market shifts, job losses, and financial instability. However, they also present openings for entrepreneurs, businesses, and individuals willing to pivot and adapt. Historically, companies like Netflix, Airbnb, and Zoom emerged stronger from economic downturns by recognizing changing consumer needs and adjusting their business strategies accordingly.

1. ***Embrace Innovation and Adaptability***
   Businesses that thrive during disruptions are those that remain agile. Being open to new ideas, technologies, and processes is crucial. This could mean digital transformation, automation, or pivoting to new markets based on emerging needs.
2. ***Identify Emerging Market Needs***
   Economic disruptions often lead to new consumer behaviors and demands. Entrepreneurs who can pinpoint these shifts and respond accordingly position themselves for success. For example, during the COVID-19

pandemic, companies that quickly adapted to e-commerce, remote work solutions, and virtual services saw significant growth.

3. ***Leverage Technology***

   Technology is often at the forefront of economic recovery. Artificial intelligence, blockchain, and data analytics are reshaping industries and creating new business models. Companies that integrate technology into their operations can streamline processes, improve customer experiences, and create innovative products.

4. ***Diversify Revenue Streams***

   Relying on a single revenue source can be risky in uncertain times. Businesses should explore multiple income streams, such as subscription services, online marketplaces, or strategic partnerships, to ensure financial stability.

5. ***Invest in People and Skills***

   Workforce development is critical during economic shifts. Investing in employee training, leadership development, and new skill acquisition prepares businesses to meet evolving industry demands. Companies that foster a culture of learning and adaptability gain a competitive edge.

6. ***Seek Strategic Partnerships***

   Collaboration can be a game-changer. Forming alliances with complementary businesses, industry leaders, or government agencies can open doors to funding, resources, and new customer bases. Strategic partnerships also enhance credibility and accelerate business expansion.

7. ***Access Capital and Funding Opportunities***
   Economic downturns often bring about funding initiatives, grants, and investment opportunities for innovative businesses. Entrepreneurs should proactively explore financing options, from venture capital to government assistance programs, to secure the resources needed to grow.
8. ***Maintain a Resilient Mindset***
   Success in uncertain times requires resilience and an entrepreneurial mindset. Viewing challenges as opportunities rather than obstacles fosters creativity and problem-solving. Leaders who remain adaptable, persistent, and focused on long-term growth will navigate disruptions more effectively.
9. ***Continuous Feedback and Self-Reflection:*** Offer regular constructive feedback and encourage self-reflection to identify areas for improvement and ensure sustainable growth

Economic disruptions are not roadblocks but catalysts for change. By embracing innovation, leveraging technology, and maintaining a resilient mindset, businesses and entrepreneurs can transform uncertainty into opportunity. Those who adapt, diversify, and strategically position themselves for the future will emerge stronger, more competitive, and poised for long-term success.

CHAPTER 3

Power Moves

From Hustle to Enterprise

In today's economy, many aspiring entrepreneurs start with a side hustle before transitioning into a full-time business. While both involve generating income independently, the long-term potential and structure of each differ significantly.

Side Hustles: Supplemental Income with Limited Growth

A side hustle is a small business or gig that individuals run alongside their primary job. It provides extra income, flexibility, and financial security but typically remains limited in scale due to time constraints and lack of infrastructure. Examples include freelance writing, selling handmade products, consulting, and ridesharing.

Key Characteristics of a Side Hustle:

- **Lower startup costs:** Often requires minimal capital and resources.

- **Limited scalability:** Growth is constrained by personal time and effort.
- **Lower risk:** Can be maintained alongside a primary job with little financial risk.
- **Personal involvement:** Success heavily depends on the entrepreneur's direct participation.

Scalable Businesses: Designed for Growth and Expansion

A scalable business, on the other hand, is structured to grow exponentially beyond the founder's direct involvement. These businesses focus on systems, automation, and team-building to expand operations and revenue without being limited by the owner's time. Examples include tech startups, e-commerce brands, subscription services, and franchises.

Key Characteristics of a Scalable Business:

- **Higher initial investment:** Often requires capital for infrastructure, staff, and marketing.
- **Growth potential:** Designed to reach larger audiences and generate significant revenue.
- **Delegation & automation:** Built with processes that allow operations to function without direct hands-on work.

- **Long-term sustainability:** Can evolve into an asset that generates passive income or can be sold.

Which Path is Right for You?

Choosing between a side hustle and a scalable business depends on your goals, risk tolerance, and available resources. While a side hustle provides immediate financial relief and flexibility, a scalable business has the potential to create long-term wealth and legacy. For those starting with limited resources, a strategic approach is to begin with a side hustle, validate the business model, and transition into scalability over time.

Shifting from survival mode to strategic thinking as an entrepreneur means transitioning from reactive, short-term decision-making to proactive, long-term planning and execution. It's about moving from a mindset of "how do I make it through today?" to "how do I build something sustainable and scalable?" Here's what that shift looks like in practical terms:

1. Financial Stability & Resource Management

Survival Mode: Scrambling to cover immediate expenses, relying on inconsistent cash flow, and making decisions based on financial desperation.
Strategic Thinking: Implementing financial planning,

creating multiple revenue streams, understanding financial statements, and managing money with intention.

2. Business Vision & Goals

Survival Mode: Operating day-to-day with no clear long-term direction, just trying to keep things running.
Strategic Thinking: Defining clear business goals, setting milestones, and developing a roadmap for growth.

3. Customer & Market Focus

Survival Mode: Trying to sell to anyone just to make ends meet.
Strategic Thinking: Identifying an ideal customer base, refining branding, and developing strong marketing strategies to attract and retain customers.

4. Operational Efficiency & Scaling

Survival Mode: Doing everything yourself, overwhelmed with daily tasks, with no automation or delegation.
Strategic Thinking: Implementing systems, processes, and automation tools, hiring or outsourcing to focus on high-value tasks.

5. Risk Management & Adaptability

Survival Mode: Constantly putting out fires, reacting to challenges without preparation.
Strategic Thinking: Identifying potential risks, having contingency plans, and being proactive about industry shifts.

6. Networking & Collaboration

Survival Mode: Operating in isolation, focusing only on short-term sales.
Strategic Thinking: Building strong relationships, forming partnerships, and leveraging connections for long-term opportunities.

7. Brand Positioning & Authority

Survival Mode: Competing on price, struggling to differentiate from competitors.
Strategic Thinking: Establishing expertise, creating high-value content, and building a brand that commands premium pricing.

8. Innovation & Growth Mindset

Survival Mode: Sticking to what's comfortable, avoiding risks, and fearing failure.
Strategic Thinking: Embracing innovation, taking

calculated risks, and continuously learning to stay ahead.

9. Leadership & Team Building

Survival Mode: Struggling with decision-making, working solo, and lacking guidance.
Strategic Thinking: Developing leadership skills, hiring the right team, and fostering a culture of growth and accountability.

10. Mental & Emotional Shift

Survival Mode: Feeling exhausted, overwhelmed, and reactive to problems.
Strategic Thinking: Cultivating resilience, self-care, and a mindset focused on abundance, solutions, and opportunities.

This shift doesn't happen overnight, but it's a necessary transformation for entrepreneurs who want to move from merely surviving to truly thriving in their business. Which areas do you feel are most relevant for you right now?

Resilience

1. **Develop a Strong "Why"** – Having a clear purpose fuels perseverance. Revisit your mission frequently.

2. **Embrace Failures as Lessons** – View setbacks as feedback, not as personal defeats.
3. **Maintain Financial Preparedness** – Create a financial buffer and multiple revenue streams.
4. **Build a Support Network** – Surround yourself with mentors, coaches, and like-minded entrepreneurs.
5. **Prioritize Self-Care** – Burnout is real. Prioritize mental and physical health.
6. **Stay Spiritually Anchored** – Faith and mindfulness can provide strength during challenges.

Adaptability

1. **Monitor Market Trends** – Keep up with consumer behaviors, economic shifts, and emerging technologies.
2. **Stay Agile in Decision-Making** – Be willing to pivot when strategies aren't yielding results.
3. **Develop Cross-Skills** – Learning new skills enhances flexibility and problem-solving.
4. **Listen to Your Customers** – Their feedback can guide necessary adjustments.
5. **Use Data to Make Decisions** – Regularly analyze key performance indicators to guide changes.

Innovation

1. **Think Beyond the Obvious** – Challenge traditional industry norms to create something fresh.
2. **Solve Real Problems** – The most successful entrepreneurs address pain points with unique solutions.
3. **Leverage Technology** – Use AI, automation, and digital platforms to optimize efficiency.
4. **Encourage Creativity in Your Team** – Foster a work culture that embraces new ideas.
5. **Collaborate with Industry Disruptors** – Partnerships with forward-thinkers can unlock new opportunities.

Developing Resilience, Adaptability, and Innovation-Survival Strategies

---

1. **RESILIENCE**: The Power of Endurance in Business

Resilience is the ability to bounce back from failures, financial downturns, and unforeseen crises. Entrepreneurs who thrive in tough times **expect** challenges and **turn obstacles into opportunities**.

Case Study: Sara Blakely – Spanx

- **Challenge**: Sara Blakely, the founder of Spanx, was repeatedly rejected by potential investors and manufacturers.
- **Resilient Action**: She refused to take "no" for an answer. Instead of giving up, she researched textile manufacturing, cold-called hosiery mills, and **invested her life savings** to launch Spanx.
- **Outcome**: Spanx became a billion-dollar company without external investors.
- **Lesson**: Entrepreneurs must **believe in their vision** and push through rejection. Tenacity separates those who make it from those who quit.
-

Resilience Strategy

✔ **Develop a "Bounce-Back Plan"**: Have contingency plans for setbacks.
✔ **Keep a Support System**: Build relationships with mentors, peers, and coaches.
✔ **Control the Narrative**: Shift failures into learning experiences rather than permanent defeats.

---

2. ADAPTABILITY: Pivot or Perish

Adaptability is staying flexible in business models, products, and strategies when markets shift unexpectedly. Entrepreneurs who succeed learn to **adjust quickly** and **embrace change**.

Case Study: Netflix – The Ultimate Pivot

- **Challenge**: Netflix started as a DVD rental service in the late '90s. When streaming technology emerged, DVD sales were declining, and competitors like Blockbuster dominated physical rentals.
- **Adaptive Action**: Instead of sticking to DVDs, Netflix pivoted into **streaming services**, ultimately forcing Blockbuster out of business.
- **Outcome**: Today, Netflix is valued at over $200 billion, revolutionizing the way people consume content.
- **Lesson**: Entrepreneurs must **anticipate industry shifts** and proactively pivot.

Adaptability Strategy

✔**Monitor Market Trends**: Stay informed about technology, customer behavior, and economic shifts.

✔ **Pivot Early**: Don't wait until the business is failing—make small, calculated changes before a crisis.

✔ **Iterate, Don't Stagnate**: Continuously test new ideas and strategies to stay competitive.

3. **INNOVATION**: Creating the Future Instead of Reacting to It

Innovation isn't just about new ideas—it's about **solving real-world problems with smarter, more efficient solutions**.

Case Study: Airbnb – Turning Crisis into Innovation

- **Challenge**: During the 2008 recession, Brian Chesky and Joe Gebbia couldn't afford their rent in San Francisco.
- **Innovative Action**: They noticed a hotel shortage in the city and rented out air mattresses in their living room as temporary accommodations for visitors.
- **Outcome**: What started as "Air Bed & Breakfast" turned into **Airbnb**, now a $100+ billion business disrupting the hotel industry.
- **Lesson**: Entrepreneurs should look for opportunities hidden inside problems and leverage underutilized resources.

Innovation Strategy

✔ **Solve Customer Pain Points**: Identify where existing services/products fail and improve them.
✔ **Think Unconventionally**: Challenge traditional

business models and create alternatives.

✔ **Leverage Technology**: Use AI, digital tools, and automation to enhance business operations.

CHAPTER 4

From Chaos to Cashflow

Low Cost With High Returns

In today's fast-evolving economy, aspiring entrepreneurs must embrace **low-cost, high-impact business models** that require minimal upfront investment yet offer scalable and sustainable success. Three of the most effective models include **Digital Knowledge Commerce**, where individuals monetize their expertise through online courses, coaching, and consulting; **Lean E-Commerce**, leveraging print-on-demand and drop-servicing to sell products or services without managing inventory; and **Community-Driven Subscription Models**, which generate recurring revenue through memberships, exclusive content, or curated product subscriptions. These models not only minimize financial risk but also maximize reach, profitability, and long-term brand influence in an increasingly digital world.

1. Digital Knowledge Commerce (Courses, Coaching & Consulting)

- **What it is:** Selling expertise through online courses, coaching, workshops, or consulting services.
- **Why it works:** Low overhead, high-profit margins, and scalable.
- **Examples:**
    - Online courses on platforms like Teachable or Udemy
    - Business or life coaching (group or 1-on-1)
    - Niche consulting (brand strategy, marketing, operations)
- **Impact Factor:** Positions the entrepreneur as an authority while providing recurring revenue through memberships or subscription-based learning.

2. Lean E-Commerce (Print-on-Demand & Drop Servicing)

- **What it is:** Selling products without maintaining inventory by using print-on-demand services or outsourcing services (like design, copywriting, or web development).
- **Why it works:** No need for upfront stock, and automation makes it scalable.

- **Examples:**
    - Print-on-demand (custom t-shirts, journals, mugs)
    - Drop-servicing (hiring freelancers to fulfill services under your brand)
    - White-labeling products (branding and reselling existing products)
- **Impact Factor:** Allows entrepreneurs to focus on marketing and brand-building while third parties handle fulfillment.

3. Community-Driven Subscription Models

- **What it is:** Membership-based platforms providing continuous value (digital or physical).
- **Why it works:** Predictable recurring revenue with engaged customers.
- **Examples:**
    - Exclusive business networks (like *Black Business Connect, Chamber of Commerce, Entrepreneurs Organize (EO)*, Business Network International (BNI)
    - Subscription boxes (grooming, wellness, or fashion)
    - Premium content/newsletter (insights, market trends, business playbooks)

- **Impact Factor:** Builds long-term customer relationships, making it easier to sustain and grow a business.

Maximizing Your Business Potential with Free and Low-Cost Tools

Starting and growing a business doesn't have to mean breaking the bank. With the rise of digital solutions, entrepreneurs now have access to a wide range of free and low-cost tools that can help streamline operations, boost productivity, and enhance marketing efforts. Whether you need help with project management, accounting, design, or communication, there are cost-effective solutions available to help you run your business efficiently without a hefty price tag. Below is a curated list of powerful tools that can give your business a competitive edge while keeping expenses low.

Essential Free and Low-Cost Business Tools

1. **Canva** – A user-friendly design tool for creating professional-looking graphics, presentations, and marketing materials.
2. **Trello** – A visual project management tool that helps teams organize tasks and workflows using boards and lists.

3. **Slack** – A communication platform that enables real-time messaging, file sharing, and team collaboration.
4. **Google Workspace (Docs, Sheets, Slides, Drive)** – A suite of cloud-based productivity tools for document creation, collaboration, and storage.
5. **Wave Accounting** – A free accounting software that offers invoicing, expense tracking, and financial reporting.
6. **Mailchimp** – An email marketing platform with automation features to help businesses manage email campaigns and audience engagement.
7. **Zoom** – A video conferencing tool that facilitates virtual meetings, webinars, and screen sharing.
8. **Asana** – A project and task management tool that helps businesses track work progress and stay organized.
9. **Hootsuite** – A social media management platform that allows scheduling, monitoring, and analytics across multiple social media accounts.
10. **Shopify (Low-Cost Option)** – A leading e-commerce platform that helps businesses set up and manage online stores.
11. **Buffer** – A social media scheduling tool that allows you to plan and automate posts for better engagement.

12. **Grammarly** – An AI-powered writing assistant that helps improve grammar, spelling, and clarity in business communication.
13. **HubSpot CRM** – A free customer relationship management (CRM) tool that helps businesses track interactions and manage leads.
14. **Evernote** – A note-taking and organization tool that helps entrepreneurs keep track of ideas, documents, and to-do lists.
15. **Dropbox** – A cloud storage service that allows businesses to store, share, and collaborate on files securely.
16. **Square** – A low-cost payment processing system for businesses that need to accept credit card payments online or in-person.
17. **Fiverr** – A marketplace to find affordable freelancers for graphic design, writing, and other business tasks.
18. **Google Analytics** – A free tool that provides website performance insights to track visitor behavior and improve marketing strategies.
19. **Notion** – A versatile workspace that combines notes, databases, and project management tools for teams and individuals.
20. **Zoho CRM** – A cost-effective customer relationship management tool that helps businesses automate sales and customer engagement.

These tools can help you save money while improving efficiency, allowing you to focus on growing and sustaining your business. Let me know if you need recommendations tailored to your industry!

CHAPTER 5

Make Dollars Make Sense

Show Me The Money

Securing funding is one of the biggest challenges for entrepreneurs, especially those in underserved communities or industries with limited access to traditional financial resources. Fortunately, creative funding options like grants, micro-loans, and community crowdfunding provide alternative ways to access capital without the burden of large debts or rigid banking requirements. These options offer flexibility and accessibility, allowing small business owners, startups, and creatives to secure the financial support they need to launch, sustain, or grow their ventures. Understanding how each works can help entrepreneurs choose the best funding path for their specific needs and business goals.

Grants are non-repayable funds provided by government agencies, private foundations, and corporations to support businesses, nonprofits, and individual entrepreneurs. Unlike loans, grants do not require repayment, but they often come with specific eligibility criteria and application processes. Some grants focus on particular industries, demographics, or social causes, making them an excellent option for minority-owned businesses, women entrepreneurs, and those in creative or community-driven sectors.

Micro-loans are small loans, typically ranging from a few hundred to a few thousand dollars, designed to help startups and small businesses that may not qualify for traditional bank loans. These loans are often provided by nonprofit organizations, community development financial institutions (CDFIs), and government-backed programs such as the SBA Micro-loan Program. Micro-loans typically have lower interest rates and more flexible repayment terms, making them an accessible option for entrepreneurs looking for a financial boost without the burden of high-interest debt.

Community Crowdfunding leverages the power of social networks and digital platforms to raise funds from individuals who believe in a business or project. Platforms like Kickstarter, GoFundMe, and Kiva allow entrepreneurs to pitch their ideas and secure funding through small contributions from a large number of supporters. Some crowdfunding models offer rewards or equity in exchange for contributions, while others operate as donation-based funding. This method not only provides financial support but also helps build a loyal customer base and validate a business concept before full-scale launch.

Each of these funding options can be strategically used based on the stage and needs of your business, helping entrepreneurs access capital without relying solely on traditional banking institutions.

The Hidden Costs of Entrepreneurship

Many aspiring entrepreneurs focus on startup capital and revenue projections but often overlook the hidden costs that can erode profits and threaten business sustainability. Failing to recognize these expenses—such as taxes, compliance fees, operational inefficiencies, and fluctuating market conditions—can lead to financial strain, cash flow issues, and even business failure. Awareness and proactive planning for these costs are essential for long-term success.

1. **Taxes & Compliance Fees** – Business taxes, payroll taxes, and state/federal compliance fees can be higher than expected.
   Preparation: Consult with an accountant to understand tax obligations and set aside a portion of revenue for tax payments.

2. **Legal & Licensing Costs** – Business permits, intellectual property protection, and contract reviews add up.
Preparation: Budget for legal fees and research necessary licenses early on to avoid penalties.

3. **Operational Inefficiencies** – Time delays, inventory mismanagement, or process bottlenecks can increase costs.
Preparation: Invest in automation and operational strategies to streamline workflows.

4. **Marketing & Customer Acquisition** – Advertising, branding, and customer retention require ongoing investment.
Preparation: Develop a long-term marketing plan with a mix of organic and paid strategies to balance costs.

5. **Employee & Contractor Expenses** – Hiring, training, and benefits for staff can be costlier than anticipated.
Preparation: Factor in salaries, benefits, and potential turnover costs when budgeting for personnel.

6. **Technology & Software Fees** – SaaS subscriptions, cybersecurity, and tech updates can be ongoing expenses.

Preparation: Audit software needs and invest in scalable solutions to avoid overspending.

7. **Supply Chain & Inventory Costs** – Fluctuations in supplier pricing and shipping fees can impact margins.
Preparation: Build relationships with multiple suppliers and maintain an emergency inventory budget.

8. **Unexpected Repairs & Maintenance** – Equipment breakdowns, office maintenance, and infrastructure failures can disrupt operations.
Preparation: Allocate a contingency fund for emergency repairs and routine maintenance.

9. **Economic Fluctuations & Market Changes** – Inflation, industry shifts, or consumer demand changes can affect revenue.
Preparation: Stay informed on industry trends, diversify income streams, and maintain an emergency fund.

10. **Entrepreneurial Burnout & Personal Costs** – The emotional, physical, and financial strain of running a business can take a toll.
Preparation: Prioritize self-care, time management, and mentorship to maintain balance and productivity.

By identifying these hidden costs early and implementing proactive financial planning, entrepreneurs can build resilience and ensure business longevity.

CHAPTER 6

Brand Like a Boss

Mind Your Matrix

Develop A Strong Brand Identity

Developing a **strong brand identity** that resonates with customers—especially in today's economy—requires a mix of **authenticity, strategy, and adaptability**. Here's how an entrepreneur can build a brand that stands out and connects deeply with their target audience:

1. Clarify Your Brand Purpose & Values

- Define what your brand **stands for** beyond making money.
- Ensure your brand aligns with today's economic and social concerns, such as **sustainability, inclusivity, and innovation**.
- Craft a **mission statement** that resonates with your ideal customer's values.
-

2. Know Your Audience & Their Pain Points

- Conduct **market research** to understand your audience's desires, struggles, and spending habits in the current economy.
- Use customer feedback, surveys, and social listening to refine your brand message.
- Adapt to economic shifts—customers today prioritize value, transparency, and convenience over luxury branding.
-

3. Create a Distinct Visual Identity

- Design a logo, color scheme, typography, and packaging that align with your brand's essence.
- Ensure all branding elements evoke the emotions you want your audience to associate with your business.
- Keep branding consistent across all platforms (website, social media, packaging, marketing materials).
-

4. Develop a Unique & Compelling Brand Voice

- Your brand voice should reflect your values and speak directly to your audience.
- Decide if your brand will be authoritative, warm, witty, educational, or aspirational.

- Make sure your messaging is relatable, inclusive, and culturally relevant to your audience.
-

5. Leverage Storytelling to Build Emotional Connection

- Storytelling is crucial in branding because it creates an emotional connection between a brand and its audience.

- Share your **brand story**—why you started, what challenges you overcame, and what impact you want to make.
- Showcase real customer stories, testimonials, and behind-the-scenes insights.
- Use **video content** to humanize your brand and make it more engaging.
-

6. Position Yourself as an Industry Expert

- Create **valuable content** (blogs, videos, webinars, e-books) that **educates** your audience.
- Collaborate with **influencers, brand ambassadors, or industry leaders**.
- Be visible on panels, podcasts, and social media discussions to establish credibility.
-

7. Build Community & Brand Loyalty

- Foster a **loyal community** through social media engagement, memberships, or exclusive content.
- Offer **personalized experiences**—custom recommendations, VIP perks, or loyalty programs.
- Leverage **user-generated content** to increase authenticity and trust.
-

8. Adapt to Economic Trends & Consumer Behavior

- With inflation and shifting priorities, focus on affordable luxury, sustainability, and convenience.
- Implement flexible pricing models, discounts, or financing options.
- Offer subscription services, bundles, or limited-time exclusives to **increase perceived value**.

9. Leverage Digital Marketing & E-commerce

- Optimize your website & social media presence for a seamless customer experience.

- Use **SEO, paid ads, and influencer partnerships** to expand your reach.
- Implement **AI-driven chatbots, virtual consultations, or augmented reality experiences** to enhance engagement.
-

10. Maintain Brand Consistency Across All Touch-points

- Ensure every customer interaction (from packaging to customer service) reinforces your brand identity.
- Keep messaging and design **consistent across all platforms**.
- Regularly **review and refine** your brand strategy based on analytics and customer feedback.

Storytelling Builds Connection

1. Emotional Connection & Trust

- People connect with stories, not just products. A **compelling brand story** makes your audience feel something—whether it's empowerment, nostalgia, or aspiration.

- When **consumers relate** to your journey, values, or struggles, they're more likely to trust and support your brand.

2. Differentiation in a Crowded Market

- The beauty and fashion industries are saturated, but **your story is unique**.
- Instead of just selling a product or service, you're selling a lifestyle, identity, and experience—which helps your brand stand out.

3. Builds Brand Loyalty & Community

- A strong narrative turns customers into **ambassadors**.
- When people resonate with your mission (e.g., celebrating big & tall men's fashion, redefining grooming for Black men), they feel like part of a movement—not just buyers.

4. Simplifies Complex Messages

- Facts and features are forgettable, but **stories stick.**
- Instead of listing ingredients in your product, you can tell a **"transformation story"**—how

proper grooming boosts confidence and self-image.

5. Drives Higher Sales & Engagement

- Emotional decisions drive purchases.
- A compelling story turns "just another beard oil" into a **legacy product**—something that speaks to the customer's identity and values.

6. Gives Your Brand a Purpose Beyond Profit

- Your journey from entrepreneur to thought leader is a powerful voice.
- **Sharing your why**—whether it's uplifting underserved communities, changing industry narratives, or promoting self-care—gives people a reason to support you.

Trust and authenticity matter more than ever in todays world—building a loyal customer base as a new entrepreneur requires a mix of personal connection, value-driven engagement, and community-building strategies. Here are some authentic and engaging ways to achieve that:

Build a Story-Driven Brand

People connect with stories, not just products.

Share:

- **Your "Why"** – What inspired your business?
- **Your Journey** – Be transparent about your entrepreneurial struggles and wins.
- **Customer Success Stories** – Feature real people who love your product.

A compelling story makes your brand memorable and relatable, fostering an emotional connection that keeps customers coming back.

2. Hyper-Personalized Customer Experience

- **Know Your Customers' Names & Needs**: Engage like a **trusted friend** instead of a seller.
- **Handwritten Notes & Thank You Videos**: Add a personal touch in follow-ups.
- **Customized Product Recommendations**: Use customer data to suggest products they actually need.

Small gestures like a personalized email or a handwritten note make a lasting impact and differentiate your brand from larger, impersonal competitors.

3. Leverage Micro-Influencers & Brand Ambassadors

- Partner with **small, relatable influencers** who align with your audience.
- Encourage loyal customers to **become brand ambassadors**.
- Offer referral incentives (discounts, exclusive access, VIP perks).

Micro-influencers often have higher engagement rates than celebrities and can introduce your brand to a niche, highly targeted audience.

4. Create a Tight-Knit Community

Customers stay loyal when they feel part of something bigger.

- **Private Facebook or WhatsApp Groups**: Exclusive discussions, early product drops, insider tips.

- **Live Q&A Sessions**: Direct engagement builds trust.

- **Local Meetups & Pop-ups**: In-person connections deepen loyalty.

A strong community fosters a sense of belonging, making customers feel like stakeholders in your brand's success.

5. Educate & Provide Value Beyond the Sale

Customers trust **brands that teach**.

- **Blog & Social Content**: Share solutions to their problems.
- **Live Tutorials & Webinars**: Show how to use your product effectively.
- **Email Tips & Guides**: Keep them engaged with useful content.

Providing ongoing education builds credibility and positions you as an expert in your industry.

6. Offer an Experience, Not Just a Product

- Create **an unboxing experience** (premium packaging, personalized note).
- Provide **VIP treatment** to repeat customers (early access, loyalty discounts).
- Make your brand **feel luxurious and intentional**.

Customers are willing to pay more for a brand that provides an unforgettable experience.

7. Prioritize Fast, Friendly, and Fair Customer Service

- Solve problems **before they complain**.
- Offer **hassle-free returns**.
- Go above and beyond—send a **free gift or surprise** when issues arise.

Excellent customer service turns first-time buyers into lifelong supporters.

8. Be Present Where Your Audience Hangs Out

- **Instagram & TikTok**: Quick, engaging reels & customer testimonials.
- **YouTube & Podcasts**: Deep dives into industry discussions.
- **In-Person Networking**: Attend events where your target audience is.

Visibility in the right places ensures that your brand stays top of mind for potential and existing customers.

9. Keep the Conversation Going with Email & SMS Marketing

- Send **regular, valuable content** (not just promotions).
- Create **a sense of exclusivity**—VIP deals only for subscribers.
- Use **personalized messaging** (e.g., birthday discounts, abandoned cart reminders).

Consistent engagement through email and SMS helps maintain customer interest and loyalty.

10. Stand for Something Bigger Than Sales

Customers support brands that **align with their values**.

- Advocate for **a cause relevant to your audience**
- Donate a % of profits to **community initiatives**.
- Show up for **causes that matter** to your audience.

Customers are more likely to stay loyal when they see your business making a positive impact beyond just selling products.

Loyalty isn't bought—it's earned. The more you show up, connect, educate, and over-deliver, the more customers will ride with you for life. **By focusing on relationships rather than just transactions,** you can build a sustainable, loyal customer base that fuels long-term business success.

CHAPTER 7

The Power of Partnerships

Networking & Collaboration

The traditional mindset of competition is giving way to a new, more powerful strategy—collaboration. Businesses, especially those led by Black and Brown entrepreneurs with limited access to capital and resources, are realizing that working together creates greater opportunities than going it alone. Collaboration fosters innovation, expands market reach, and strengthens industry influence, all while reducing operational costs and risks. In a disrupted economy where agility and adaptability are key to survival, partnerships and strategic alliances have become the new currency of success. The future belongs to those who understand that collective growth outpaces individual rivalry.

Entrepreneurs can leverage community resources and collective economics by tapping into the power of shared networks, collaborative funding, and localized support systems. By engaging with their communities, business owners can access mentorship, shared knowledge, pooled financial resources, and group purchasing power, all of which reduce operational costs and create sustainable growth. Strengthening economic ties within a community not only supports individual business success but also uplifts the entire local economy.

Ways to Leverage Community Resources and Collective Economics:

1. **Join Local Business Associations & Chambers of Commerce** – Network with other entrepreneurs and gain access to funding, training, and promotional opportunities.
2. **Collaborate with Other Small Businesses** – Share spaces, split marketing costs, or create co-branded products and services.
3. **Tap into Community-Based Crowdfunding** – Utilize platforms like GoFundMe or local investment pools to raise capital.
4. **Partner with Nonprofits & Social Enterprises** – Gain access to grants, sponsorships, and community support for business initiatives.
5. **Use Cooperative Purchasing** – Pool resources with other businesses to get bulk discounts on inventory, services, or equipment.

6. **Engage in Bartering & Skill Exchange** – Trade services with other professionals to minimize expenses.
7. **Participate in Local Pop-Up Markets & Vendor Events** – Increase brand visibility and sales through community-driven marketplaces.
8. **Access Public & Private Business Incubators** – Leverage free or low-cost office space, mentorship, and funding resources.
9. **Advocate for Community Banking & Credit Unions** – Work with local financial institutions that prioritize funding for small businesses.
10. **Educate & Employ Locally** – Offer training programs, hire from within the community, and create pathways for economic mobility.

Your relationship with your suppliers and vendors is crucial to the success of your business. Here are some key ways business owners can build strong, beneficial relationships with suppliers and vendors:

1. Communicate Clearly and Consistently

- Set clear expectations regarding product quality, delivery schedules, and pricing.
- Use multiple communication channels (email, calls, meetings) to stay aligned.

- Provide constructive feedback and be open to suggestions.

2. Negotiate Fairly but Strategically

- Approach negotiations as a partnership rather than a battle.
- Aim for win-win pricing and payment terms that work for both parties.
- Explore bulk purchasing or long-term contracts for better deals.

3. Pay On Time (or Early, If Possible)

- Timely payments build trust and may open doors for better terms in the future.
- Some suppliers offer discounts for early payments—take advantage of these if feasible.

4. Develop Personal Relationships

- Get to know your key contacts and build rapport.
- Attend industry events or supplier-hosted gatherings to strengthen connections.
- Send occasional thank-you notes or holiday greetings to show appreciation.

5. Be Loyal to Reliable Suppliers

- Consistency in orders helps vendors prioritize your needs.
- A long-term relationship can lead to priority treatment during shortages or peak demand.

6. Be Transparent About Business Needs and Challenges

- If cash flow is tight or demand is fluctuating, be upfront with your suppliers.
- Honesty can lead to flexible payment plans or customized solutions.

7. Collaborate on Innovation and Improvement

- Work together on new product development or cost-saving ideas.
- Give suppliers insights into market trends so they can better serve your needs.

8. Diversify Your Supplier Network but Maintain Core Partnerships

- Having multiple suppliers reduces risk, but maintaining strong relationships with a few key ones ensures reliability.

- Keep a balance between supplier loyalty and having backup options.

9. Support Their Business Growth as Well

- Refer other businesses to reliable suppliers.
- Share positive reviews and testimonials when appropriate.
- Offer insights on how their products/services can be improved.

10. Use Technology for Efficiency

- Implement digital payment systems, automated ordering, and tracking tools.
- Utilize supplier relationship management (SRM) software to streamline interactions.

CHAPTER 8

Digital Domination

Leveraging Technology for Growth

The Power of an Online Business

In today's digital age, the power of an online business is undeniable. Unlike traditional brick-and-mortar stores, an online business offers low overhead costs, global reach, and 24/7 availability, making it an attractive option for entrepreneurs with limited resources. The rise of e-commerce, social media marketing, and digital payment solutions has leveled the playing field, allowing small businesses to compete with larger corporations.

An online business allows for flexibility, automation, and scalability. Whether it's selling products, offering services, or monetizing content, digital platforms provide opportunities for entrepreneurs to create multiple revenue streams with minimal upfront investment. With the right strategy, an online business can generate passive income, build brand authority, and create financial independence.

1. Advice for Setting Up an Online Business with Minimal Cost

1. **Find a Profitable Niche** – Focus on a niche market where there is demand but low competition. Identify a problem and provide a solution through your products or services.

2. **Use Free or Low-Cost Platforms** – Start with platforms like Shopify (free trial), Etsy, Gumroad, or WooCommerce (if you have a WordPress site) to sell products. Service-based businesses can use Upwork, Fiverr, or LinkedIn.

3. **Leverage Social Media for Marketing** – Instead of paid ads, use organic social media marketing. Build an audience on platforms like Instagram, TikTok, Facebook, and LinkedIn by sharing valuable content.

4. **Build a Simple Website or Online Store** – Use free website builders like Wix, WordPress, or Canva Websites to create a professional-looking site with minimal cost. Having a website adds credibility.

5. **Utilize Dropshipping or Print-on-Demand** – If selling physical products, avoid inventory costs by using dropshipping (e.g., via

AliExpress, Spocket) or print-on-demand services like Printful.

6. **Create Digital Products or Services** – E-books, online courses, coaching, consulting, or subscription-based memberships require little to no upfront investment but can generate substantial income.

7. **Use Free Marketing Strategies** – Focus on SEO (Search Engine Optimization), blogging, podcasting, and email marketing with tools like Mailchimp (free plan) to build an audience.

8. **Leverage AI and Automation** – AI-powered tools like ChatGPT, Canva, and Buffer can help automate content creation, customer service, and marketing without hiring staff.

9. **Partner with Influencers or Affiliates** – Instead of paying for ads, collaborate with micro-influencers in your niche for exposure in exchange for free products or commissions.

10. **Start Lean and Scale Gradually** – Begin with a minimal viable product (MVP), test the market, and reinvest profits into growing your business.

By focusing on digital-first strategies and leveraging free resources, anyone can start an online business with minimal cost. The key is consistency, creativity, and a strong understanding of your audience's needs.

Utilizing E-Commerce, Automation, and AI Tools for Business Success

In our digital economy, leveraging e-commerce, automation, and artificial intelligence (AI) is essential for entrepreneurs looking to streamline operations, increase efficiency, and scale their businesses. This chapter explores leading strategies to harness these tools for success.

2. E-Commerce Strategies for Growth

Multi-Channel Selling – Expanding beyond a standalone website to platforms like **Amazon, Walmart Marketplace, eBay, and Etsy** increases visibility and sales potential.

Subscription & Bundling Models – Offering auto-replenishment options and curated product bundles enhances customer retention and boosts sales.

Personalized Shopping Experiences – AI-driven product recommendation engines help businesses upsell and cross-sell products based on customer behavior.

Live Shopping & Social Commerce – Platforms like **Instagram, Facebook Live, and TikTok Shop** provide opportunities for real-time engagement, product demonstrations, and instant purchases.

AI-Powered Chatbots & Virtual Assistants – AI chatbots like **Tidio, Drift, or Chatfuel** improve customer service by answering FAQs, recommending products, and handling common inquiries 24/7.

Augmented Reality (AR) for Virtual Try-Ons – Retail businesses can use **Zakeke or Vue.ai** to allow customers to visualize products before purchasing, reducing return rates and enhancing satisfaction.

Dynamic Pricing Strategies – AI-driven pricing tools like **Prisync or Wiser** help monitor competitors and automatically adjust prices for optimal profitability.

3. Automation for Business Efficiency

AI Email Marketing & Retargeting – Tools like **Klaviyo, Mailchimp AI, or Omnisend** automate personalized email campaigns for abandoned carts, restock alerts, and customer engagement.

Social Media Content Scheduling & AI Copywriting – Platforms like **Buffer, Later, and Hootsuite** automate posting schedules, while AI tools like **Jasper or Copy.ai** generate compelling captions, blogs, and ads.

Automated Inventory & Order Fulfillment – Third-party logistics (3PL) providers like **ShipBob, Fulfillment by Amazon (FBA), and Printful** handle warehousing and shipping, reducing manual workload.

AI-Powered CRM (Customer Relationship Management) – Platforms like **HubSpot AI, Zoho CRM, or Salesforce Einstein** track customer interactions, sales data, and purchasing patterns to optimize marketing strategies.

Smart Review & Feedback Collection – AI-driven reputation management tools such as **Yotpo or Trustpilot AI**automatically collect customer reviews, helping businesses build trust and credibility.

Loyalty & Referral Programs – AI-powered loyalty systems (Smile.io, Yotpo Loyalty) increase customer retention and word-of-mouth marketing through personalized rewards.

4. How to make use of AI

AI-Driven Market Research – Platforms like **Google Trends, ChatGPT AI analytics, and Semrush** provide real-time insights into industry trends, consumer behavior, and competitor strategies.

Automated Financial Management – AI tools such as **QuickBooks AI, Xero, or Bench** track revenue, categorize expenses, and provide predictive financial analytics.

AI Chatbots for Customer Support & Sales – AI-powered virtual assistants (Zendesk AI, Gorgias) handle customer queries, process returns, and provide product recommendations in real time.

Predictive Analytics for Inventory & Demand Forecasting – AI software like **Brightpearl AI or NetSuite** helps businesses optimize stock levels, preventing overstocking and shortages.

AI-Powered Ad Optimization – Platforms like **Google AI Ads, Facebook AI Ads, and Adzooma** automatically refine ad targeting, improving return on investment (ROI) for digital marketing campaigns.

5. Integrating AI & Automation into Various Business Models

For E-Commerce & Retail Businesses:

- AI-driven product recommendations enhance customer experience.
- Automated order tracking and fulfillment reduce manual errors.
- AI-powered trend analysis helps businesses stay ahead of seasonal demand.

For Personal Brands & Content Creators:

- AI-assisted book marketing & sales tracking (BookBolt, Reedsy AI) optimize book sales.
- AI-powered course creation tools (Teachable AI, Thinkific AI, Kajabi) streamline online education.
- Automated podcast & video transcription (Descript AI, Otter.ai) make content creation more efficient.

For Service-Based Businesses & Coaching Programs:

- AI chatbots assist with scheduling and customer inquiries.

- AI-driven CRM tools personalize client interactions.
- Automated invoicing and billing platforms improve cash flow management.

Steps for Implementation

1. **Assess Business Needs** – Identify pain points where **automation and AI** can improve efficiency, reduce costs, or enhance customer experience.
2. **Choose the Right Tools** – Select platforms that integrate with existing systems to minimize disruptions.
3. **Start Small, Scale Gradually** – Begin with **automating repetitive tasks** such as emails and inventory management before expanding into AI-driven personalization and analytics.
4. **Monitor & Optimize Performance** – Use AI-powered analytics tools like **Google Analytics AI, Tableau, or Looker Studio** to track key performance indicators (KPIs) and adjust strategies as needed.

The Future of Business: AI & Automation as Growth Catalysts

Embracing AI, automation, and e-commerce innovations is no longer optional—it's a necessity for sustainable business growth. By leveraging these technologies, entrepreneurs can enhance efficiency, improve customer engagement, and scale their ventures with greater ease.

This chapter serves as a foundation for understanding how digital tools can transform a business in a rapidly changing economy. Entrepreneurs who adopt these strategies will be well-positioned for long-term success.

Understanding where the real money is when comparing digital products versus physical products is crucial for strategic growth. Digital products—such as online courses, e-books, subscription services, and software—offer high profit margins, scalability, and low overhead, making them attractive for entrepreneurs seeking passive income and global reach. In contrast, physical products—like clothing, skincare, and consumer goods—require inventory management, logistics, and production costs but provide tangible brand presence, customer loyalty, and diversified revenue streams. The key to success lies in aligning your business model with the advantages of each, leveraging digital for automation and scalability while strategically incorporating physical products for brand impact and market authority.

When evaluating the profitability of digital versus physical products for entrepreneurs, several key factors emerge from industry analyses and case studies.

Profit Margins and Scalability: Digital products, such as e-books, online courses, and software, typically offer higher profit margins due to minimal production and distribution costs. Once developed, these products can be sold infinitely without significant additional expenses, allowing for easy scalability and global reach. In contrast, physical products involve costs related to manufacturing, inventory management, and shipping, which can reduce profit margins and complicate scaling efforts.

garynealon.com

Market Trends and Growth Projections: According to Statistica, the digital transformation of business practices, products and organizations is projected to reach 2.8 trillion in 2025. This surge is driven by increased internet adoption and a growing preference for online solutions. Physical products continue to dominate overall consumer spending; however, the complexities associated with production and distribution can pose challenges for entrepreneurs, especially in terms of scalability and adapting to market fluctuations.

whop.com & statistica.com

Case Studies: Entrepreneurs focusing on digital products have reported significant success. For instance, a Sweden-based band increased their profit margin by 45% and gross profits by 500% by selling their music directly to consumers online. Similarly, individuals offering online courses and digital memberships have built substantial income streams with relatively low overhead costs.
podia.com

Challenges: Despite the advantages, digital products face challenges such as market saturation and issues related to intellectual property protection. Physical products, while offering tangible value and potentially lower return rates, require more complex logistics and higher upfront investments.
blog.varstreetinc.com

Over the next decade, the trend towards digital products is expected to continue, driven by technological advancements and consumer preferences for immediate, accessible solutions. Entrepreneurs aiming for higher profitability and scalability may find digital products to be a more advantageous focus, provided they navigate the associated challenges effectively.

Cybersecurity- What's The Big Steal

Cybersecurity is crucial for **protecting your business** online because cyber threats are constantly evolving, targeting businesses of all sizes, particularly small and minority-owned enterprises that often lack robust defenses. A breach can lead to financial loss, identity theft, data exposure, and damage to your company's reputation, potentially crippling operations.

Cybercriminals use phishing attacks, ransomware, and data breaches to exploit vulnerabilities, making it essential for entrepreneurs to implement strong passwords, secure networks, data encryption, and regular software updates.

Investing in cybersecurity not only **safeguards** sensitive business and customer information but also ensures compliance with legal regulations, builds trust with clients, and fortifies your business against costly cyberattacks. Proactive protection is no longer optional—it's a necessity for business survival in the digital economy.

CHAPTER 9

The Resilience Factor

Staying The Course

Entrepreneur's Unshakable Foundation

The journey of an entrepreneur will challenge your confidence, push your limits, and present obstacles that seem insurmountable. Faith becomes the anchor that keeps you steady when uncertainty looms, reminding you that purpose is greater than profit. It fuels your belief in what is unseen, giving you the courage to take risks, pivot when necessary, and trust that the work you are putting in today will manifest in due time. Discipline is the backbone that transforms dreams into realities, requiring you to show up, stay consistent, and refine your craft even when motivation wanes. Without it, ideas remain just ideas, and success remains a distant wish.

But it is perseverance that truly separates those who make it from those who don't. Every entrepreneur will face setbacks—failed deals, financial struggles, moments of doubt—but resilience is built in the decision to keep going despite the hardship. The most successful business owners are not the ones who never failed, but the ones who refused to quit. They adapted, learned from their mistakes, and kept moving forward. As you navigate this entrepreneurial journey , let your faith keep you grounded, your discipline keep you focused, and your perseverance carry you through every challenge. Because in the end, success is not just about making money—it's about overcoming the odds and proving to yourself that you were built for this. It is this mindset that builds legacies, transforms industries, and creates lasting impact.

Mental Health & Self-Care:

Entrepreneurship is already a high-stakes game, but for those in underserved communities—where access to funding, mentorship, and institutional support is limited—the stakes are even higher. Every setback can feel like a major roadblock rather than a minor bump in the journey.

For Black and Brown entrepreneurs, especially those launching businesses with minimal resources, the weight of systemic barriers, financial instability, and social expectations can take a deep mental and emotional toll.

Without intentional mental health and self-care practices, these challenges can lead to burnout, decision fatigue, and in some cases, abandoning the dream altogether. But when properly nurtured, mental resilience can help entrepreneurs push past failures, learn from setbacks, and develop the long-term stamina needed to succeed.

1. Navigating Financial Pressure & Scarcity Mindset

For many entrepreneurs especially those in underserved communities, lack of access to capital is the number one challenge. Without generational wealth or easy access to business loans, many are forced to bootstrap their businesses, often relying on personal savings, family support, or high-interest loans. The pressure to "make it work" with limited financial safety nets can lead to chronic stress, anxiety, and self-doubt.

- **Mental Resilience Tip:** Shift from a *scarcity mindset* to a *resourcefulness mindset.* Instead of focusing on what you lack, focus on creative ways to leverage what you have—whether it's bartering services, seeking community funding, or collaborating with other entrepreneurs to pool resources.

2. Overcoming Systemic Barriers & Discrimination

Entrepreneurs of color frequently face systemic barriers, including limited access to bank loans, lower approval rates for business credit, and fewer networking opportunities with high-level investors. Discrimination—whether implicit bias in funding decisions or exclusion from key business spaces—can create frustration, imposter syndrome, and mental exhaustion.

- **Self-Care Tip:** Instead of internalizing these barriers as personal failures, recognize them as systemic issues. Join Black- and Brown-led entrepreneurial networks, community-based business accelerators, and culturally aligned financial institutions that are committed to leveling the playing field. Surround yourself with a support system that understands your journey.

3. Balancing Business, Family, & Community Expectations

Many entrepreneurs are not just building businesses—they're also supporting families, working multiple jobs, and juggling community responsibilities. The expectation to succeed not just for themselves but for their families and communities can create immense pressure.

- **Stress Management Tip:** Set **boundaries** between your business, personal life, and community obligations. It's okay to say no. Make space for yourself without feeling guilty. Prioritizing self-care allows you to serve others more effectively in the long run.

4. Battling Entrepreneurial Loneliness & Lack of Mentorship

Many underserved communities lack accessible mentorship programs, incubators, or experienced entrepreneurs who can provide guidance. Without mentors or role models who have successfully navigated similar paths, it's easy to feel alone, unsupported, and uncertain about next steps.

- **Connection Tip:** Seek peer support groups, online communities, and mentorship networks specifically designed for Black and Brown entrepreneurs. Even if your local area lacks resources, virtual platforms can provide mentorship, advice, and connections that help you stay motivated.

5. Dealing with Fear of Failure & High Stakes Risks

For many, entrepreneurship is not just about personal ambition—it's often a race to economic mobility and ending generational cycles of poverty. Because of this, failure is not an option. The fear of making a costly mistake can lead to avoiding taking risks, hesitation in decision making , and missed opportunities.

- **Mindset Tip:** Reframe failure as *data* rather than *defeat.* Each mistake is a way to see what doesn't work, to better understand what does. Small failures are stepping stones to big success.

6. Coping with Mental Fatigue from Constant Hustling

Many Black and Brown entrepreneurs feel pressured to constantly be in *hustle mode*, working long hours without rest. The cultural expectation of non-stop grit and grind can be both a strength and a weakness. Without intentional breaks, you experience a decline in creativity, mental fatigue, and the inability to make crucial decisions.

- **Self-Care Tip: Reject the toxic hustle culture.** Rest is a revolutionary act. Taking time off is a business strategy, not laziness. Schedule mental recharge days, prioritize sleep, and engage in activities that restore your energy.

7. Healing from Generational Trauma & Financial Anxiety

For many entrepreneurs of color, financial instability isn't just a personal issue—sometimes it's generational. Growing up in households where money was always tight creates deep-seated financial anxiety that can make entrepreneurship feel like a constant survival battle rather than a growth opportunity.

- **Healing Tip:** Seek financial literacy education tailored for underserved entrepreneurs. Shift from a survival mentality to a wealth-building mindset. Work with culturally competent financial coaches or business advisors who understand the unique financial challenges you face.

8. Maintaining Clarity and Sound Decision-Making

Stress and exhaustion impair cognitive function, making it difficult to think strategically, solve problems, and innovate. Entrepreneurs who practice self-care—through activities like exercise, therapy, or even a short mental break—are better equipped to approach challenges with a clear and focused mind.

- **Clarity Tip:** Schedule time for solitude or reflection each week. Stepping away from work allows you to return with fresh insights and renewed energy.

Mental Well-Being is a Business Survival Tool

For entrepreneurs in underserved communities, success isn't just about grit and strategy—it's also about mental resilience, emotional well-being, and self-care.

By prioritizing mental health, setting boundaries, finding community, and shifting limiting mindsets, entrepreneurs can overcome setbacks, recover from failure, and build businesses that not only survive—but thrive.

In a disrupted economy where resources are scarce, your most valuable asset isn't just money—it's your mindset, your emotional endurance, and your ability to keep going despite the odds.

Mindful Resilience: Meditation Practices to Help Overcome Setbacks

Entrepreneurship is a journey filled with challenges, failures, and unexpected setbacks. To navigate these obstacles with clarity and confidence, incorporating meditation practices into your daily routine can help manage stress, improve decision-making, and cultivate resilience. Here are key meditation techniques tailored for entrepreneurs facing adversity:

1. **Prayer**
   - Prayer fosters inner peace, resilience , and clarity by connecting the mind, body, and spirit. It reduces stress, strengthens faith and cultivates gratitude. Pray provides guidance & renewed strength.

2. **Mindful Breathing (Box Breathing or 4-7-8 Method)**
   - A simple yet powerful practice where you inhale for four counts, hold for seven, and exhale for eight. This

technique calms the nervous system, reduces anxiety, and helps regain focus after setbacks.

3. **Visualization for Success**

   ○ Close your eyes and visualize yourself overcoming challenges, learning from failures, and achieving your business goals. This practice rewires your brain for resilience, reinforcing a growth mindset.

3. **Body Scan Meditation**

   ○ Bringing awareness to different parts of the body helps entrepreneurs release tension and stress that accumulate from daily pressures. This practice improves relaxation and physical well-being.

4. **Loving-Kindness Meditation (Metta Meditation)**

   ○ By focusing on self-compassion and extending goodwill toward others, this meditation helps entrepreneurs overcome self-doubt, disappointment, and frustration associated with failure.

5. **Journaling & Gratitude Meditation**

  - Start or end your day by reflecting on three things you're grateful for. Pairing gratitude with deep breathing reinforces a positive outlook and shifts focus from failure to opportunity.

6. **Mantra Meditation for Confidence**

  - Repeating affirmations such as *"I am capable," "Every setback is a setup for success,"* or *"I am resilient"*helps entrepreneurs silence negative self-talk and stay motivated.

7. **Walking Meditation for Mental Clarity**

  - A mindful walk, focusing on each step and breath, can provide mental clarity, spark creativity, and offer fresh perspectives on business challenges.

By incorporating these meditation techniques, entrepreneurs can develop the mental strength to bounce back from failures, manage stress effectively, and maintain a clear vision for success.

CHAPTER 10

Scaling Smart

Growing Without Overextending

Scaling up means focusing on what you do best and delegating the rest. A successful entrepreneur is not the one who does everything but the one who ensures everything gets done efficiently. Here's a breakdown of key business functions that should be automated and outsourced to help entrepreneurs scale efficiently:

Key Functions to Automate

Automation helps reduce repetitive tasks, improve efficiency, and ensure consistency. Here are the top areas where automation is essential:

1. Customer Relationship Management (CRM)

- Use tools like HubSpot, Zoho, or Salesforce to track leads, automate follow-ups, and manage client interactions.

- Automate email sequences and responses for inquiries.

2. Marketing & Social Media Management

- Schedule social media posts using platforms like Buffer, Hootsuite, or Later.
- Automate email marketing through Mailchimp, ConvertKit, or Klaviyo.
- Use chatbots for common customer inquiries on websites and social media.

3. Financial Tracking & Invoicing

- Automate bookkeeping with QuickBooks, FreshBooks, or Wave to track income and expenses.
- Use invoicing software to send reminders for unpaid invoices.

4. E-commerce & Order Fulfillment

- Automate inventory tracking and payment processing using Shopify, WooCommerce, or Square.
- Use fulfillment services like ShipBob or Amazon FBA for logistics.

5. HR & Payroll Processing

- Automate payroll with Gusto, ADP, or Paychex to ensure compliance and on-time payments.
- Use hiring tools like LinkedIn Recruiter or BambooHR to screen candidates efficiently.

Key Functions to Outsource

Outsourcing allows entrepreneurs to focus on strategy and growth while leveraging expert services. The following functions should be delegated to specialists:

1. Legal & Compliance

- Hire an attorney or legal service (e.g., LegalZoom) to handle contracts, trademarks, and regulatory issues.
- Ensure tax compliance by working with a CPA rather than struggling through it alone.

2. Graphic & Web Design

- Contract freelancers from Fiverr, Upwork, or 99designs for branding, website development, and promotional materials.
- Focus on a polished, professional digital presence rather than DIY design.

3. Public Relations & Media Outreach

- Work with PR firms or specialists to craft media campaigns, secure interviews, and expand brand credibility.

4. Content Creation (Photography, Videography, Copywriting)

- Invest in high-quality product photography and brand storytelling through freelance content creators.
- Outsource blog writing and copywriting to ensure professional and engaging content.

5. Customer Service & Virtual Assistance

- Delegate customer support through virtual assistants or outsourcing firms.
- Use outsourced call centers or chatbot AI to handle FAQs and appointment scheduling.

6. IT & Cybersecurity

- Hire managed IT services to maintain security, website functionality, and system backups.
- Ensure protection against cyber threats with dedicated IT professionals rather than handling it internally.

Final Wisdom: When to Automate vs. Outsource?

- **Automate** when the task is repetitive, requires consistency, and doesn't need human creativity or judgment.
- **Outsource** when the task requires expertise, creativity, or strategic decision-making.

for the overachieving entrepreneur, time management is not just about productivity—it's about sustainability. Here are some effective time management skills that can prevent burnout and encourage prioritization.

1. Prioritize Like a Leader (The Eisenhower Matrix)

This method helps entrepreneurs **focus on what truly matters**:

- **Urgent & Important:** Do these tasks immediately.
- **Important but Not Urgent:** Schedule these for later.
- **Urgent but Not Important:** Delegate these.
- **Neither Urgent nor Important:** Eliminate them.

This prevents overachievers from getting stuck in "busy work" instead of high-impact activities.

2. The 80/20 Rule (Pareto Principle): *Work Smarter, Not Harder*

- **80% of results come from 20% of efforts.** Identify and focus on **high-yield** activities.
- Let go of **perfectionism** in lower-priority tasks.

3. Time Blocking: Own Your Schedule

- Set **specific time slots** for essential tasks.
- Protect time for **creative and strategic work.**
- Include **breaks** to avoid mental fatigue.

4. The Two-Minute Rule: *Reduce Procrastination*

- If a task takes **less than 2 minutes,** do it immediately.
- If it's longer, **schedule** it.
  This keeps minor tasks from piling up and overwhelming the entrepreneur.

5. Batching Similar Tasks: *Improve Efficiency*

- Group tasks by category (emails, calls, content creation, etc.).
- Eliminates **task-switching fatigue.**
- Encourages **deep focus** rather than scattered multitasking.

6. Delegate & Automate: *Free Yourself for Bigger Goals*

- Identify tasks that can be **outsourced or automated** (e.g., social media scheduling, bookkeeping, admin work).
- Invest in **AI tools, virtual assistants, and SOPs** to streamline processes.

7. The Power of Saying 'No'

- Overachievers tend to overcommit.
- Set boundaries by **aligning decisions** with long-term goals.
- Use a polite but **assertive approach** when declining distractions.

8. Strategic Rest & Recovery: *Avoid Burnout*

- Schedule **intentional downtime** (even if it's 15 minutes).
- Prioritize **sleep, nutrition, and movement** to maintain peak performance.
- Engage in **non-work activities** to refresh creativity (reading, music, meditation).

9. Review & Adjust: *Weekly Check-in*

- Reflect on what worked and what didn't at the end of each week.
- Adjust **strategies and workflows** accordingly.

CHAPTER 11

The Legacy Lives On
Building Generational Wealth & Giving Back

The Power of Ownership: The Key to Lasting Wealth

Imagine this: Two individuals start their careers at the same time. One spends 40 years working diligently in a 9-to-5 job, earning a stable income but never truly owning anything beyond personal assets. The other chooses to build a business, navigating the challenges of entrepreneurship while creating something that can grow, evolve, and outlive them. Fast forward to retirement—one relies on savings and Social Security, while the other enjoys multiple streams of income, owns valuable assets, and has a legacy to pass down. The difference? **Ownership.**

Business ownership isn't just about making money—it's about building something that lasts, something that works for you even when you're not actively working. For underserved Black and Brown communities, where wealth gaps persist due to systemic barriers, entrepreneurship is one of the most powerful tools for breaking cycles of economic hardship and creating generational stability. But wealth isn't just about money—it's about **control, freedom, and impact**.

1. Ownership Creates Equity & Long-Term Asset Growth

Unlike employment, where income stops when you stop working, owning a business means you're building **equity**—a financial asset that appreciates over time. A well-run business increases in value, making it an **asset that can be sold, franchised, or leveraged for further financial gain.** When you own a business, you're no longer just trading time for money—you're investing in something that can multiply beyond your direct effort.

Consider **Oprah Winfrey, Jay-Z, or Madam C.J. Walker**—they didn't just work for money, they created brands, ownership, and intellectual property that continue to generate wealth long after their initial work was done. **Business equity is a foundation** for financial independence and long-term wealth creation.

2. Generational Wealth & Legacy Building

A job pays for the present, but a business can provide for generations to come. The wealthiest families in the world sustain their riches not through salaries but through business ownership and investments passed down to their children and grandchildren.

For many marginalized entrepreneurs, breaking the generational wealth gap starts with creating businesses that can be inherited or used as a financial stepping stone for future generations. The more businesses we own, the more **we control our economic future**, rather than relying on external employers or unstable job markets.

3. Multiple Revenue Streams & Financial Security

One of the biggest advantages of entrepreneurship is the ability to **diversify income streams**. A business can have multiple branches—such as products, services, digital content, speaking engagements, franchising, or real estate investments.

- **A barber** can expand by selling haircare products, online tutorials, or opening multiple locations.

- **A fashion designer** can license their designs, create a signature fragrance, or collaborate with major retailers.
- **A consultant** can launch an online course, write books, or develop a membership community.

More revenue streams mean more financial security, even in unpredictable economic conditions.

4. Tax Benefits & Financial Leverage

The tax code favors business owners over employees. As an entrepreneur, you gain access to:

- **Deductions** for business expenses (travel, home office, meals, etc.)
- **Depreciation benefits** (writing off assets over time)
- **Investment tax breaks** when reinvesting in business growth

Additionally, businesses create financial leverage—allowing owners to secure business loans, purchase property, and invest in other ventures using their company as collateral. This is how wealth multiplies.

5. Community Economic Development & Job Creation

Entrepreneurship **empowers communities** by circulating money locally. When a business thrives, it creates jobs, hires from within, and reinvests in local development. Instead of relying on outside corporations, communities can **build their own economic ecosystems**, fostering financial independence and resilience.

Historically, **Black Wall Street in Tulsa, OK** was a prime example of how entrepreneurship led to **prosperous, self-sufficient Black communities**. Today, we have the opportunity to **rebuild those economic strongholds** through business ownership.

6. Business as a Platform for Investing & Wealth Expansion

Owning a business is just the beginning—it becomes a **launchpad for greater investments.**

- Profits can be reinvested into **real estate, stock markets, tech startups, or private lending**.
- Business owners can **acquire additional businesses, form partnerships, or launch nonprofit initiatives** to create long-term impact.
- Many multimillionaires start with one business and use its success to **fund other wealth-generating assets.**

Entrepreneurship is the foundation, but **smart investing ensures wealth continues to grow.**

7. Control Over Financial Destiny

Perhaps the most important reason to own a business is **control**. When you work for someone else, they dictate your hours, salary, and career trajectory. But as a business owner, you:
✔ Control your **income potential**
✔ Set your own **schedule & work-life balance**
✔ Have the power to **pivot & adapt to market changes**

In an economy where **automation, layoffs, and AI are disrupting industries**, entrepreneurship is one of the best ways to **stay ahead of financial uncertainty** and take ownership of your future.

Final Thought: Playing the Long Game in Wealth Creation

Business ownership is not just about personal success—it's about shifting economic power into our hands. For Black and Brown entrepreneurs, creating sustainable wealth means embracing ownership, leveraging financial tools, and building businesses that serve generations.

Wealth is built by strategic moves, not just hard work. If you're serious about achieving financial independence and leaving a legacy, the entrepreneurial game is one you must learn to play—and win.

Teaching Financial Literacy to the Next Generation

We often hear the phrase, "*They don't teach this in school,*" when it comes to financial literacy. The truth is, wealth isn't just about how much you make—it's about **how well you manage, grow, and sustain it**. Without financial literacy, even a successful business or high income can lead to financial instability.

For **Black and Brown communities**, where generational wealth gaps persist due to historical and systemic economic barriers, **teaching financial literacy early is a game-changer**. It equips the next generation with **the tools to break cycles of poverty, manage money wisely, and create long-term financial security**.

Here are some **practical, engaging, and culturally relevant ways** to teach financial literacy to the next generation:

1. Start with Financial Conversations at Home

What to Teach:

-The basics of **earning, saving, spending, and investing**

-The importance of **credit, budgeting, and avoiding debt traps**

-How **entrepreneurship** creates wealth beyond a paycheck

How to Teach It:

✔ Normalize money discussions at the dinner table. Ask kids, *"If you had $100, what would you do with it?"* and guide them toward smart financial choices.

✔ Share **real-life financial stories**—good and bad—to give them context.

✔ Encourage **goal setting**, like saving for a bike, a laptop, or a business idea.

Example: A father who owns a barbershop can explain how profit works, why rent and supplies cost money, and how reinvesting in the business leads to growth.

2. Give Kids Real Money to Manage

What to Teach:
-The value of **saving before spending**
-The impact of **small investments over time**
-How to make **money work for you**
How to Teach It:
✔ Give kids an allowance or earnings from small jobs, but **tie it to responsibility** (e.g., they must save at least 20% before spending).
✔ Open a **youth savings account** and show them how interest works.
✔ Introduce **financial goal-setting** (e.g., saving for a toy, a business, or an investment).

Example: A mother gives her son $10 a week but requires him to:

- **Save $3**
- **Give $1 to charity or family support**
- **Invest or set aside another $1 for long-term goals**

By doing this, the child **learns budgeting, generosity, and future planning**.

3. Introduce the Power of Investing Early

What to Teach:
-The difference between saving and investing

-The basics of stocks, real estate, and business investments
-Why ownership creates wealth over time

How to Teach It:
✔ Use kid-friendly stock apps (like Greenlight, BusyKid, or Stockpile) to show how stocks grow.
✔ Let teens **invest in small shares** of major companies they recognize (Nike, Apple, Tesla, etc.).
✔ Play **investment games** or use real money to teach **risk vs. reward**.

Example: A family challenges their kids with a $100 stock market experiment—they pick stocks, track performance, and learn how money grows through investment.

4. Teach Entrepreneurship Through Hands-On Experience

What to Teach:
How to create, market, and sell a product or service
The difference between being a worker vs. an owner
How to scale a business from an idea to profit

How to Teach It:
✔ Encourage kids to start a small business (lawn care, selling crafts, tutoring, baking, reselling sneakers).

✔ Help them budget their earnings, track profits, and reinvest in their idea.
✔ Use **social media** to introduce branding and marketing skills.

Example: A young girl who loves baking sells homemade cookies at school events. She learns:

- **Pricing** (covering ingredients and making a profit)
- **Marketing** (creating a brand, word-of-mouth sales)
- **Growth strategy** (reinvesting profits into better packaging or advertising)

By running a micro-business, kids learn financial skills in real life, not just theory.

5. Make Financial Learning Fun & Engaging

What to Teach:
Money management doesn't have to be boring—it should be interactive and empowering.

How to Teach It:
✔ Play money-based board games (Monopoly, Cashflow, The Game of Life).
✔ Watch financial literacy cartoons (like *Cha-Ching* or

Warren Buffett's Secret Millionaires Club).
✔ Challenge kids with budgeting exercises (e.g., "Plan a $500 vacation" or "Design a $100 grocery list").

Example: A father plays **Monopoly** with his kids but adds **real-life money lessons** like:

- *"This is how property investing works."*
- *"You lost money because you didn't budget for rent!"*
- *"Now you see why banks charge interest."*

By making money tangible and fun, kids become financially literate without realizing they're learning.

6. Teach the Importance of Credit & Debt Early

What to Teach:
Credit scores impact housing, business loans, and financial freedom.
Bad debt traps (credit cards, payday loans) vs. good debt (homeownership, business loans).

How to Teach It:
✔ Give teens a secured credit card to build responsible credit habits.
✔ Show them how credit scores work using their own

family's examples.
✔ Explain interest rates with practical examples.

Example: A teenager who wants a car must research loan rates, insurance, and monthly payments before being allowed to finance one. This teaches debt responsibility before adulthood.

Building Financially Smart Future Generations

Financial literacy isn't just about numbers—it's about empowerment. If we want to close the wealth gap and create true economic independence, we must teach financial responsibility early, encourage ownership, and equip young people with real-world financial tools.

By shifting the next generation's mindset from *spending to investing, working to ownership, and consuming to creating,* we set them up for long-term success, financial freedom, and generational wealth.

The earlier financial literacy is taught, the more it becomes a lifelong habit. Wealth isn't built overnight—but when the next generation understands money, it lasts for generations.

Trending Industries for Entrepreneurs

Based on recent analyses, the top industries where new small businesses are being formed include:

1. **Retail Trade**: Encompassing both traditional brick-and-mortar stores and the rapidly expanding e-commerce sector, retail trade remains a leading industry for small business formation.
   guidantfinancial.com
2. **Food and Restaurant Services**: This sector continues to attract entrepreneurs, with many venturing into niche markets such as food trucks, specialty cafes, and catering services.
   guidantfinancial.com
3. **Health, Beauty, and Fitness Services**: The growing consumer focus on wellness has led to a surge in businesses offering health-related services, including gyms, spas, and beauty salons.
   guidantfinancial.com
4. **Construction and Contracting**: With increasing demand for residential and commercial development, many small businesses are emerging in construction,

renovation, and related contracting services. guidantfinancial.com

5. **Professional and Business Services**: This broad category includes consulting, marketing, legal, and other professional services that support businesses across various industries. guidantfinancial.com

6. **Information Technology**: The IT sector encompasses software development, cybersecurity, and tech consulting, with small businesses playing a crucial role in driving innovation. biz2credit.com

7. **Manufacturing**: Small-scale manufacturing, particularly in specialized or artisanal products, has seen growth, contributing significantly to local economies. biz2credit.com

8. **Transportation and Warehousing**: The rise of e-commerce has increased the need for logistics, leading to the formation of small businesses in delivery, freight, and warehousing services. biz2credit.com

9. **Educational Services**: There's a growing demand for tutoring, test preparation, and vocational training services, prompting

entrepreneurs to establish educational ventures.
guidantfinancial.com

10. **Accommodation and Food Services**: This sector includes hotels, motels, and other lodging services, alongside food service establishments, catering to both locals and tourists.
biz2credit.com

These industries have been identified based on factors such as average revenue, funding approval rates, and overall growth potential for small businesses.

Brand Identity Development Worksheet

This worksheet is designed to provide clarity and direction for building a strong, resonant brand identity. Need further guidance? Let's strategize together

Section 1: Define Your Brand Purpose & Values

1. What is the mission of your brand? (What do you aim to achieve?)

2. What are the core values that define your brand? (E.g., authenticity, sustainability, inclusivity)

3. What problem does your brand solve for your customers?

Section 2: Identify Your Target Audience

4. Who is your ideal customer? (Age, gender, income level, interests, etc.)

5. What are their biggest pain points?

6. How does your brand meet their needs?

Section 3: Develop Your Brand Voice & Messaging

7. Describe your brand's personality in three words.

8. What tone of voice will you use? (Friendly, professional, humorous, inspiring, etc.)

9. Write a short brand tagline or slogan that encapsulates your message.

Section 4: Visual Identity 10. What are your brand's primary colors?

11. What fonts or typography will represent your brand?

12. Do you have a logo concept? (Sketch or describe it below.)

Section 5: Storytelling & Emotional Connection

13. What is the story behind your brand? (Why did you start it? What inspired you?)

14. How do you want customers to feel when they interact with your brand?

15. What unique experiences or values set you apart from competitors?

Section 6: Brand Positioning & Marketing

16. Where will you market your brand? (Social media, website, retail, events, etc.)

17. What are your key marketing strategies? (SEO, influencer collaborations, content marketing, paid ads, etc.)

18. How will you measure brand success? (Sales, customer engagement, social media reach, etc.)

Section 7: Customer Loyalty & Community Building

19. How will you engage with and retain customers? (Loyalty programs, exclusive content, personalized experiences, etc.)

20. How can you create a sense of community around your brand?

Next Steps:

- Review and refine your answers.
- Use this worksheet to develop a cohesive brand strategy.
- Implement branding elements consistently across all platforms.
- Continuously evaluate and adapt based on customer feedback.

REFERENCES

The Personality Tree- Florence Littauer (Author)

Britannica.com

wikipedia.org

Talkroute

The strategy story- Sept 12, 2020

The Business Mogul Matrix *is a movement in a time and space that requires entrepreneurs to step up and take action. It's either pivot or perish there is no in-between. The path to economic freedom and entrepreneurial success is within reach, but it requires knowledge, strategy, and persistence. It's time to prepare your business to win.*

Mrs Walker is available for speaking engagements and business development platforms. Fell free to contact her at: myra@MyraWalkerEnterprises.com

If this book has helped you in any way, please share this journey with a fellow entrepreneur, friend or co-worker and encourage them to get their copy by scanning the code on the next page.

ABOUT THE AUTHOR

Myra Walker has been on the front lines of the fashion industry for more than three decades. She is as an award winning fashion designer, writer and business executive. Myra is on a crusade to equip and encourage Entrepreneurs to walk in their greatness. She is touching the lives of small business owners and organizations across the nation with her motivational message and ***The Business Mogul Matrix*** Movement. She facilitates empowerment seminars, business workshops and educational programs globally. Ms Walker is dedicated to the empowerment of the next generation of entrepreneurs and has captivated a loyal, diverse audience through her various social media outlets, Educational Board assignments, and speaking platforms. She is the advocate for every person to live a healthy, abundant, successful life. She is a native of Long Beach, California, a world traveler and lives bi-coastal.

Made in the USA
Columbia, SC
07 March 2025

54807263R00070